EXTREME

BUSINESS

BUILDING

From Concept to Profit in 60 Days

Mary L. MacNeilly

EXTREME BUSINESS BUILDING
Copyright © 2012 by Mary L. MacNeilly

ISBN-13:978-1478210726

ISBN-10:1478210729

Printed in USA

Dedication

This book would not have been possible without the fabulous mentors and influences in my early career. I'm often asked how I could possibly know everything I know, at such a young age. My answer is simple. I've learned how to leverage my passion, competitive spirit, and thirst for knowledge to grow into an experienced business professional, by listening, trusting, and absorbing wisdom and knowledge from my mentors and influences.

This book is dedicated to them: Mark Sayre, Jarred Brown, Sarah Sinicki, Jim Casart, David Block, Lisa Michaud, Helen Omar, Eric Reamer, Dr. Leif Stephens, and the many more that have helped along the way.

Lastly, my loudest cheerleader and biggest fan is my Yiayia. She passed away one week before this book was sent to be printed. Her passing has inspired me even more to reach new levels and be thankful for everything that comes my way.

To all of you, thank you.

Table of Contents

Preface

I began my professional career at age 21 when I realized that bartending and teaching dance was not exactly going to pay my bills forever. I did not have a college degree. I did not have business acumen. I did not even know how to use a fax machine. What I did know is that I had passion.

A mortgage company offered me a receptionist position, and I am surprised I was not fired within the first week of starting the job. I had never answered a multi-line phone, sorted mail, or been responsible for so many tasks. But, I persevered and started to learn how a business operates.

After ten months, I was fed up with the industry and was offered a position with Paychex, Inc. as a sales assistant. I first met Mark Sayre, the District Sales Manager, during my second interview. I knew then my life was about to change. Additionally, the $29,000 salary offer was a $6,000 increase for me and I was elated!

Mark was the first and most influential individual in my professional career. No one had believed in me and saw so much potential in me, as he did. He invested his time and energy into developing me over five years. During this time, I earned a college degree, was promoted twice, increased my compensation six times, held the #1 sales rep title (for my role) twice, crushed sales records, was asked to be a speaker and trainer multiple times for reps and managers, and had the opportunity to work directly with the VP of the $300 million division of the $2 billion company on infrastructure, systems, and process discussions.

My opportunity with Paychex, Inc. changed my life. I quickly moved on to start working with startup companies. Grow, LLC had been operating for several years when I joined their team. Jim Casart, Sarah Sinicki, Jarred Brown, and I worked closely together to rebuild this business from the ground up. Within months, the company started to double, triple, and quadruple revenue.

My next opportunity was with Helen Omar at Wyoos.com. My knowledge expanded immediately upon accepting a position with her. I became her right-hand woman and built the infrastructure, systems, and processes for the business within 30 days.

After only four short months with Helen, I realized that my passion was building businesses. I had figured out how to build an entire business, with multiple revenue streams, and a clear roadmap to success in just days. It was time for me to start my own business so I could build multiple businesses at one time. And that is what I do today!

I began writing this book after helping build business #5 in June of 2012. I realized there a lot of very expensive business consultants out there that give decent advice, but I had yet to find a business builder that spoke the down and dirty truth to their clients. My nickname is 2x4 Mary because there is no fluff when working with me. You want a profitable business? Then listen up, commit, and follow the steps in this book to building a business worth owning!

Introduction

Congratulations! You want to be a business owner. That is fantastic. Good for you. Has anyone told you how difficult it is? Have you tried before and failed? What happened? Did you create a business plan? Did you follow it? Did you build a team or try to do it by yourself?

These are all great questions you should ask yourself when you decide to build a business. The quicker you realize that building a business takes time, energy, money, passion, *and* failure, the quicker you can build a business worth owning.

The best advice I ever received about starting a business came from my friend and owner of Actuate Social, Lisa Michaud. It went something like this:

We all have natural talents. Something we just happen to be good at doing. But seldom are our natural talents our passion. When building a business, most of us take the easy road and build the business on what we happen to be good at doing, not necessarily what we love.

When you build a business and you're not in love with it, one of two things will happen. You'll either get bored, no matter how profitable or successful it is, and choose to start over or go down a new path. Or you will choose to run a business for a lifetime that drains you and never gives you the satisfaction of being a business owner.

So don't be the business owner who goes to bed at night and questions the path they chose. Make a list of what you LOVE to do and build a plan to achieve it. It may not be the easy path, but it will be the path with the greatest reward.

These words changed my entire outlook on the original business plan for my business, The Butterfly Creative, LLC. For those who have already been in business or have already developed your concept, read that passage again, let it soak in, and ask yourself what changes you need to make to your business concept/plan before you begin reading this book.

It's alright to think that it is extra work or much harder to achieve the business you *really* want. I promise you, if you believe in it, it is not out of reach. So take the time now to decide what you are really passionate about and love. If you do not happen to be perfect at it, don't worry. That is why we build teams.

Two of my influencers said it best. When asked what attributed most to his success, Mark Sayre responded, "I only surround myself with the *best* people". And when Dr. Leif Stephens was asked what motivates him to work hard no matter what, he replied, "When you know what you want, the sweat doesn't matter".

All templates mentioned in this book are available to download on our website, www.thebutterflycreative.com. We recommend you use them; however you can create your own…

Chapter One – Am I in Love with My Business?

The first exercise you need to do is ask yourself if you are in love with your business, or business concept (if you haven't created the business yet). But what does being in love with your business actually mean?

You will notice that business is like dating. My first example: creating and committing to a business is a big investment. Just like committing to another person in a relationship. When you are looking to date someone, you have "knock-out factors" or "deal breakers," if you will. List your knock-out factors now for your business. What is a deal breaker for you? Perhaps break them into categories for simplicity; type of customer, volume, revenue, resources required for producing product, estimated amount of your involvement, need for employees/additional personnel resources, and/or capital needed to start the business.

To help with this exercise, I've included a list below.

Customer	My Time	Capital	Revenue
Big ego	More than 80 hours/week	Need more than $5k to start	Make less than $100/hr.
No money	Conflicts w/ family time	Need more than $5k monthly cushion	Push less than 50% to the bottom-line
Bad attitude	Being "tied" to business		

Once your list is built, take a minute to ask yourself if you are starting or have created a business that contains any elements on your knock-out list. This is a great starting point to identify some changes that, by being made now, can save you a lot of time, energy, and money in the long run… just like building a strong foundation for a house or for a marriage.

Now let us look at the definition of passion versus what you happen to be good at doing. In an effort to best explain this, I am going to tell you my story of when I built my business.

Per the advice I received from Lisa Michaud (mentioned in the introduction), I made a list of everything I loved to do. I built a business that had five "buckets". I included one on one consulting, outsourced lead generation (telemarketing), outsourced sales, event planning/coordination (as a marketing method), and teaching dance. Clearly they were not all related, but I loved doing each one. I built my business off these five buckets. I created my time management calendar to ensure I could fit them all in, I set up revenue tracking systems to be able to monitor my key performance indicators (like income per hour), and I was ready to go!

I knew I had too much on my plate, but I promised myself that after three months, I would evaluate each bucket and choose two buckets to continue. Well, three months went by and I chose my two buckets. Another month went by, and I asked myself the same question I've asked you. Am I in love with my business? I was working well over 80 hours per week, one bucket was sucking up my time, only producing $2,000 a month over 160 hours ($12.50 per hour), and the other was producing $5,000 per month over 50 hours per month ($100 per hour). But wait, that's only 210 hours per month. I was working about 320 hours. Where was the other 110 hours being spent?

This was the first part of my exercise and I encourage you to do the same if you're currently operating a business. You might be surprised by the results. I found my time was being spent on managing my employees, networking, and sitting through coffee meeting after coffee meeting with people I should have never been sitting with, but we will discuss this later.

Now back to the story. I asked myself if I was in love with my business. I was not in love with the hours or income, but I was happy. I asked myself what made me happy, and I realized my passion is to be great at what I do. My passion was not one on one consulting or outsourced lead generation. It is knowing that I am good at and effective with what I do. I am great at building businesses! So here came the next question. If my passion is being good at what I do (building businesses), how can I impact more small business owners, but work less hours, and make more money?

The day I answered that question is the day I immediately changed by business model. I realized that I absolutely love speaking and training. I then combined the two passions, speaking/training and building businesses, and now I have a business worth owning!

After you answer the question, think about what changes you can make immediately. Think about the changes you should make, but are hesitant to, and why. Write them out. List out why they cannot be changed today and put together a timeline of when they can be changed. Once you have decided what your passion is and what you love to do, read on and start the next chapter.

Chapter Two – Let's Start Building!

Once you have your concept in place, write out your mission and vision. The mission is about why you and your company are doing what you are doing. It is about how you affect your audience, market, the economy, the planet, and so on. Make it relevant and heartfelt. Your mission is the start to your marketing messaging and can be used in a variety of ways to create and support your brand. Your vision is just that; your vision. Where do you see your company 2, 3, or 20 years from now? Are you an industry leader? Will you solve an economic crisis or social issue? Tell your audience and competitors in your vision statement who they can expect your company to be. Make it a short, one sentence vision.

Now that your mission and vision are complete, let us look at your company objective. Write out a paragraph, like an introduction to your audience, on the company. Include information such as: when/where/why your company was founded and by who, the market need and market opportunity for what you do, and your differentiating factors. Now, you may not know your competition or the market need very well yet, but this is a good place to start.

Once your company objective is complete, take a moment to write out a paragraph or two to describe in detail your product or service. Hopefully, you have more than one. If you do not, do not worry. We will go through that exercise in Chapter 3. When you write about your products/services, be specific.

My example is: I provide 60-90 days' worth of in-depth business building knowledge and consulting (including templates, resources, and roadmaps) in an eight hour crash course built specifically for committed entrepreneurs who are ready to build a business worth owning. Each attendee receives a copy of my book, a workbook, 8 business building templates (including a business/operating plan, pro forma, marketing brochure, video/web marketing layout, investor slide deck, and more). Additionally, I invite my students to subscribe to The Butterfly Coaching for weekly live business building Q&A boardroom sessions, hundreds of business tips and resources, and access to my library of templates and tools.

Now, I have other revenue streams, but those are my main products/services. You should focus on one or two main products/services that you actively market and promote to your audience. However, creating a business worth owning means creating a business that you love; that makes money while you sleep, and most importantly, allows you to go on vacation!

Chapter Three – Show Me the Money!

There are four important revenue streams in business. You need to find a way to make money through ALL of them. The table below names, defines, and illustrates each type.

Revenue Stream	Payment Terms	Example
Immediate	Payment Due When Service Rendered	*Onsite training fee; billable at $85/hr., payment due upon completion of training.*
Short Term	Payment Due Bi-Weekly or Semi-Monthly	*Project-based work; total project est. at $4k over 2 mos., client pays $1k/2 wks.*
Long Term	Monthly Payment Due on Net 15 or Net 30	*Monthly consulting fees; hours totaled for month prior, to be paid within 30 days of receipt of invoice.*
Residual	Recurring Payment Due Monthly	*Monthly subscription to services; clients' credit card is auto-billed monthly.*

Create your own table like the one above and list out four ways you can make money. Each revenue stream is important to building your business because all of us want the opportunity to step away from the business and ensure its still making money! Building your business with this format creates the opportunity for you to make money while you sleep and be able to take that vacation you have been thinking about for a while now!

Additionally, should anything ever happen to you regarding your health or ability to work, building a business with this structure of financial stability will protect you in most cases. All small business owners should have a workers' compensation policy as well as short term and long term disability policies on them. Discuss purchasing a rider with your insurance agent that reduces the window of payment. Most disability insurance coverage requires a 3-6 month window before payment is issued. Be sure your business is built with these four revenue streams to protect your income and your employees in case of emergency!

Some small business owners struggle to find four ways they can ask for payment. While you are completing this exercise, understand that your end user (your client) does not have to know how you make money. Actually, no one does. Find ways to create these additional revenue streams using verticals, revenue shares, and the internet.

Here is an example. As small business owners, we all need a website. Additionally, we all sell to a target market. There are hundreds of businesses also selling into that same target market. Find a non-competing industry that is selling into your target market and offer paid advertising on your website. These strategically placed partners are viewed as a value-add to your audience, but they are making you money! Set up these advertisers on auto-billed recurring monthly billing.

Accepting payment is always a sticky situation. Asking for money is not easy for many of us. Create client agreements that are clear, concise, and ensure every client signs one! Many times, we do business with our friends and family. They are no exception! In fact, friends and family are the worst offenders when it comes to not paying invoices. Contracts and agreements can be set up in a variety of ways, but be sure the following is included:

1) Clearly written section on how fees are calculated
2) Clearly written section on when payment is due
3) Clearly written section on how payment can be made
4) Clearly written section on scope of services
5) Clearly written section on terms of agreement
6) Clearly written section on terms of past due payments

The recurring theme here is obviously "clearly written". Many agreements and contracts are too wordy and leave room for different interpretations. Make sure both parties understand the agreement in its entirety. Many times you'll find yourself in a position to have to check on payment status as many small business owners do business with other small business owners. Many small business owners have cash flow issues. Do not be a victim of accounts receivable! Depending on the scope of work, try asking for a 50% deposit or a retainer for services. Lastly, under no circumstance should you give out your services for free. Discounts? Maybe. Protect your time! Show your value from the first day you do business. *Sample agreements are available to download on our website.*

Chapter Four – Who is Doing What I'm Doing?

This section begins the market analysis summary and competitive landscape journey. Small business owners say they are unique. When asked with whom they compete, they often say, "No one really does what I do. I mean, several business do {*insert industry specific work here*}, but I do it better, I'm more experienced, and I have better technology and customer service". Trust me; there are lots of people out there doing what you are doing in your <u>target audiences' eye</u>. Your target audience is the pool from which you gain clients. They are not the industry expert on what you do! To them, you may look the same as the next guy in your industry. And trust me again, stop saying you're unique. We are all unique. Use compelling marketing messaging to explain your differentiating factors to your target audience.

One of my clients provides an online resource portal geared towards a specific demographic. Several differentiating factors existed. Yet, after every presentation, we heard, "So you're like Facebook for older people". The target audience decides who you are and what you do. Not you. The quicker you realize that your target audience tells you what you sell by expressing what they want to buy, the quicker you will see profit. Do not be surprised if your business model changes slightly every day. A successful business changes constantly until brand recognition and credibility are created. The changes slow once you are an established brand name to a large audience. But it may take years to get there, so be prepared to change your business based on what your target audience wants. Listen to them.

When conducting your market analysis summary and competitive landscape, be detailed and thorough. Use primary research techniques, not just secondary. Secondary research techniques are easier and faster. Most popular is using the Internet to find relevant information on your industry and competitors. Be sure to do your own market research. Use surveys, polling techniques (through social media or local networking groups, as an example), and focus groups. Primary research is very powerful when approaching an investor, potential client, and/or strategic partner.

An example is: "When a local focus group comprised of 110 people that match the demographic of your target audience was polled, 89% indicated they would like to see health insurance related information at the time they purchased life insurance". If I am the life insurance agent looking to build a new revenue stream by asking a health insurance agent to advertise on my website for a low recurring monthly fee (hint, hint!), this information is very useful and compelling!

The market analysis summary should be detailed and thorough and include the below information.

Market Analysis Summary
1) Market Segmentation
2) Target Market Summary
3) Market Trends
4) Market Growth
5) Market Needs
6) Main Competitors

Market segmentation refers to looking at the total market in that you can sell and segmenting out specific groups of people that will best identify with what you are selling. Target market refers to the specifics of that group. You will need to examine several factors. The factors can be broken into two categories, demographic and psychographic. Demographic elements include age, gender, race, average household income, and geographic location. Psychographic factors include lifestyle, beliefs, religion, and philosophies.

Market trends are very important. You must understand the market from a buyer behavior standpoint. Who is buying this type of product/service that you're selling? Is it a need or a want? Is it flashy and cutting edge, or a remake of a classic? The market trends will indicate how apt your target market is to buy what you sell. An example of market trends is as follows. For my business, the market trend shows that hundreds of people start businesses every day in my market. This is caused by an increase in unemployment, advancements in technology, and just an overall trend of entrepreneurship. Because of this, my target audience is growing and they seek information on how to build their business quickly and effectively so they can begin making money as quickly as possible!

Market growth shows you what the long term opportunity is for your product or service. If your target audience is an endangered species or a "dying trend", if you will, you only have so much time to market yourself and sell. Identify the growth patterns with your market. Let's say you sell online advertising. As of January 2012, more than 50% of all advertising spend was reported to be through the Internet in some capacity. That is a staggering statistic! And because of the market trends with advances in technology, the market growth is anticipated to be significant and increase consistently year over year.

Market needs must be identified within the market. Every small business owner swears their target audience *needs* their product/service. But is the market ready for you? Do trends show that the market is in need of what you provide? Have you identified a social issue, an economic opportunity, or simply listened to the market trends and identified what buying behaviors are indicating at this time? An example of a market need is anyone marketing to Baby Boomers. 70 million Boomers exist. 10,800 retire every day. The market is swelling with aging Boomers. As they age, they face transition. The psychographic research shows many lose energy, lack purpose, and do not have access to tools and resources to have a fun and meaningful life. Companies that target this demographic must understand the market need exists and create services/products that help them engage in their life, but also provide tools, resources, and education. The market has shown that only 1.5% of retiring Boomers have enough money in their retirement plan to cover 27+ years of retired living to take them to the new expected life expectancy age. Ask yourself, what is your market need?

The competitive landscape needs to be very detailed. Under number 6 above, list out the top five or six competitors you have found. When you start the competitive landscape, you need to build a competitive analysis table. An example of this table for a services based company is shown next, followed by an example of a tech-based company. Please note these are simply short examples. Professional competitive analysis tables contain much more data and can be pages in length. Additionally for tech-based companies, they are typically followed by images of the competitors' websites.

Services-Based Company

Competitor	Pricing	Services	Yrs. In Business
ABC Company	$200/hr Flat Rate	Business Consulting (operational, leadership, executive)	1 year
DEF Company	$150/hr. Flat Rate	Business Consulting (sales/marketing focused)	7 years
GHI Company	Multiple Packages $500/mo. - $2,000/mo.	Business Consulting (packages cover all functions: finance, operations, tech, sales/marketing)	2 years
JKL Company	Min. Monthly Rate of $1000/mo.	Business Consulting (legal, executive; retainer required)	12 years

Tech-Based Company

Competitor	US Ranking	Bounce Rate	Monthly Unique Visitors	Visitor Demographics
ABC Tech Company	547,629	53.6%	910k	70% Female 45-60 yrs old $72k income
DEF Tech Company	952,447	58.2%	257k	59% Female 40-50 yrs old $52k income
GHI Tech Company	2,112,389	68.7%	36k	82% Female 52-69 yrs old $46k income
JKL Tech Company	194,634	22.9%	5.2M	75% Female 45-60 yrs old $75k income

Once you have created your competitive analysis table, start listing out the main differentiating factors you see. Easy categories to start with are years of experience, specific product or services offered, end user experience, pricing, and customer service. Once your list is completed, conduct a SWOTT analysis exercise. It's important that you go through these steps first before you build a business plan or pro forma.

Chapter Five – How Am I *Really* Different?

This next section allows you to understand not what you sell, but what your clients and/or audience <u>wants</u> to buy from you. Dale Carnegie has a fantastic sales exercise in the "How to Sell Like a Pro" class. The instructor holds up an everyday object and asks the students to shout out what they're really buying when they buy that object. Below are some examples.

Camera = Memories
Chocolate = Satisfaction
Hole Puncher = Holes

How does this relate to your business? Here are some examples:

Accounting Services = Peace of Mind
Personal Trainer = Confidence, Self-Esteem
Real Estate = A Lifelong Dream

Completing a SWOTT analysis table allows you to write out exactly how you're different, why your clients/audience would want to buy from you, your areas for improvement, market opportunities, potential threats to your business, and trends (buying behavior, economy, technology) that will impact your business. SWOTT stands for:

S – Strengths
W – Weaknesses
O – Opportunities
T – Threats

T – Trends

When you create the table, label the top columns with SWOTT. On the left hand side, label the rows with the different areas of your business. You will quickly find several areas of differentiation, areas of opportunities, knowledge and management team gaps, and market opportunities (growth opportunities) for your company. I recommend including the following rows:

1) Product/Service (list each separately)
2) The Company
3) Your Messaging (see below) & Mission

You may want to consider additional fields such as technology, if it is not your main product or service, and personnel, if you would like to break it out from the company section.

The next step in understanding how to communicate your differentiating factors is first understanding how your target audience needs to be spoken to in order to be heard. In the previous section, you identified your target audience.

Let's dig deeper into the demographic and psychographic factors to understand how they need to be spoken to. My demographic and psychographic factors are the factors that you have, because you're my target audience. I had to figure out how to speak to you in my messaging so you would buy my book and attend my class. I know that you're scared. I know you put a lot on the line to start a business. I know that you have a lot riding on the success of your new business. I know there is a lot of business and sales training material out there coupled with a saturated selection of business consultants. But you came to me. Ask yourself why? What was my message? How did it resonate with you? Look at all the products/services you buy. Why did you buy them? How did that company speak to you through their messaging?

A good way to start crafting your messaging is to look at your competitors. Do not recreate the wheel here. Find out who the top three competitors are and analyze their messaging across all their channels. Pay attention for these:

1) Channel or method of communication (radio, TV, print)
2) Tone of message (fear, happiness, excitement, sadness)
3) Length of message (15/30 second ad, full print article)
4) Frequency of message (every commercial break, printed in every publication, social media blast weekly)
5) Diversity of channels (how many places/channels do you hear or see this company?)
6) Call to action (what do they ask their audience to do? Register for an event, visit a website, order online?)

Use the list above as a checklist or outline to create your messaging. When creating a messaging campaign, be sure that your messaging is consistent. Start creating your brand by saying the same sentence or couple of sentences in your advertising, marketing, on your website, on your social media channels, as an example. Allow your audience to identify with you through consistency. Creating a strong integrated marketing communications campaign allows your audience to ask, "Who is this person? I have seen them everywhere and heard about them several times! They must be good. I should call them." Or maybe you are in an industry that serves people based on chance, like an auto collision repair center. You obviously cannot market to them to have them come in unless they have a car accident. So find a way through messaging to be on their mind when they need you!

Make sure you test your messaging with your target audience. Trust me, you know <u>way</u> too much about what you do! And NO ONE CARES. They only care about what is in it for them! Speak to them! It took me a month to realize I had to shorten my messaging. When people asked what I did, I said, "I work with the management teams of startups and small businesses to help them create or redefine their overall business model through infrastructure, systems, processes, and then help them create competitive sales and marketing plans that will bring in significant new revenue to the company; ultimately creating a business worth owning!"

Wow. That was a lot. In my head, it made sense. But I would have my audience just nod their head and say it sounded wonderful. But when I realized that I should be the business expert, not them, I changed my intro to, "I build businesses; from concept to profit". Then I have their attention. Then they want to know more. "Build businesses? What kind of businesses? What kind of success have you had? Can you help me with my business?" Trust me on this, less is more! If you tell them too much through your messaging, you allow them to make a premature decision on whether or not they need you. Give a little, and watch them be attracted to you.

This method works no matter what channel of communication you use. Again, keep your messaging consistent. Keep the text short on your website. All messaging is a call to action! Do not give them everything up front. Simply indicate through your messaging what they're next step is!

Chapter Six – The Dreaded Business Plan

Yes. You need one. Yes. It needs to be detailed. No. You do not need to carry it around and show everyone. Yes. You need to keep it updated. Yes. Your business changes all the time. Yes. It can be time consuming keeping it up. But – the last time I checked, without a plan in place, a *working* plan in place, how are you held accountable for your direction and growth?

Investors, business partners, and family do not need to see this document. I teach how to create full business plans that act as operating plans and financial models. This section provides you with an outline of what a strong business plan should include. For investors, business partners, and family, we will discuss how to create a two page executive summary in the next chapter.

To begin, create a nice cover page. You may have an investor or business partner that wants to view the entire document. Brand it. Make it look professional. Place your logo on the front center of the cover page. Underneath, in a large, clear font, write "Official Business Plan Document". Add a footer that shows your company name, the title of the document, page number, and the date. All of The Butterfly Creative templates have already been created in this format. I recommend keeping the consistently with this format across all your documents. The second page needs to be a non-disclosure agreement. Just make it short and simple. Most NDAs do not even hold up in court anymore, but it is helpful to have one to show the legitimacy of your project. It can be short. Be sure anyone who receives a copy of your plan signs one of these.

The third page shows your table of contents. I recommend using headers and numbers. Your plan can get very long, very quickly. This format allows you to flip to certain sections easily. I have created several business plans for several companies. I use this exact same format every time. You'll notice that several of these sections have already been discussed in this book. However, many items listed below have not been covered. We'll walk you through each one in this chapter.

The table of contents follows.

When creating your business plan, do not be afraid to elaborate on certain sections. Using visuals and mapping out ideas through flow-chart type structures can be very helpful exercises to you to ensure you understand your product/service, market, competition, and differentiating factors. When you get to sections regarding future products, growth, personnel plans, and milestones, do not hold back. Close your eyes and envision your company one year, two years, or even five years from now. Visualize it and write down every detail. When we take the time to visualize our success and document it, we are much more likely to reach our goals.

Alright, here we go and describe each section of the business plan. Next we describe each section of the business plan. Feel free to skip past some of the sections we have already covered, or reread if you're ready for a refresher. We will cover everything in this chapter except Section 1.0, the Executive Summary and Section 8.0, the Financial Plan.

> 1.1 Objectives – The objectives section can be written out in bullet point format. It contains the key objective points that the company needs to achieve to be successful. For an Internet business, this section would include daily unique visitors, bounce rate information, and other measurements of consumer traffic and the conversion to revenue (however that happens in the business).

> 1.2 Mission - The mission is about why you and your company are doing what you're doing. It's about how you affect your audience, market, the economy, the planet, and so on. Make it relevant and heartfelt. Your mission is the start to your marketing

messaging and can be used in a variety of ways to create and support your brand.

1.3 Keys to Success - The keys to success are three main points that sum up what you, your company, and your product/service must do or deliver to ensure your company's success.

2.0 Company Summary – The company summary is a short paragraph of 3-4 sentences that summarizes who founded the company, why, and what market need you solve.

2.1 Start-up Summary - The start-up summary is more specifically detailed on what the company needs financially, operationally, and logistically to startup. This section is typically two paragraphs and includes a startup expenses table that shows all costs associated with creating and launching the company. The startup expenses table will also be used for the executive summary and use of funds summary if seeking a capital investment.

2.2 Company Ownership – The company ownership section is one paragraph that names all founders, their percentage of ownership, and their title.

3.0 Products and Services – This section is a short, 2-3 sentence summary of the main products and services.

3.1 Product and Services Description – The product and services description section gives you the opportunity to list, in detail, all your products and services. List every revenue stream as well.

3.2 Competitive Comparison – This short competitive comparison section is the first time you name your competition. List them out separately and write about 4 paragraphs on how they are currently solving the market need. Be sure to point out their strengths and weaknesses.

3.3 Sales Literature – The sales literature section is a short paragraph of 5-6 sentences that describes all types of sales literature you will need to create for your business. Describe the marketing brochures, slicks, business cards, and collateral along with your plan on how and when it will be created.

3.4 Sourcing – Sourcing refers to distribution channels of your product/service. For some industries, this is a difficult section to complete because multiple channels do not exist. Write out a short paragraph that explains through what or whom your product/service can be distributed or sold if more than one exists.

3.5 Technology – This section is the first overview of your technology requirements. Use this section to create a visual ROM (rough order of magnitude), SDLC (systems and development life cycle), and outline of your technology. Most businesses are now building mobile apps, tablet apps, mobile websites, and a standard website as part of their technology suite. Include high-level information on all these.

3.6 Future Products – The future products section is the perfect section to illustrate your dream! Use this space to describe in a couple of paragraphs the potential of where this company can go! Think about adding more revenue streams, enhancing the current product, or aligning with strategic partners to create the best must-have product or service.

4.0 Market Analysis Summary – This summary should contain a detailed overview of what sources were accessed for the primary and secondary research; cited within 2-3 paragraphs of the market need and market opportunity description. This overview should state numbers, statistics, and facts from research.

4.1 Market Segmentation - Market segmentation refers to looking at the total market in that you can sell and segmenting out specific groups of people that will best identify with what you sell. This section can be extremely detailed; include multiple sections and sub-sections.

4.2 Target Market Summary - Target market refers to the specifics of that group. There are several factors that need to be examined. The factors can be broken into two categories, demographic and psychographic. Demographic elements include age, gender, race, average household income, and geographic location. Psychographic factors include lifestyle, beliefs, religion, and philosophies. Use this section as a summary though, and provide a 2-3 short paragraph synopsis.

4.2.1 Market Trends - Market trends are very important. You must understand the market from a buyer behavior standpoint. Who is buying this type of product/service that you sell? Is it a need or a want? Is it flashy and cutting edge, or a remake of a classic? The market trends will indicate how apt your target market is to buy what you sell. You can summarize your market trends in a short, 4-5 sentence paragraph.

4.2.2 Market Growth - Market growth shows you what the long term opportunity is for your product or service. If your target audience is an endangered species or a "dying trend", if you will, you only have so much time to market yourself and sell. Identify the growth patterns with your market. Summarize the patterns and opportunity in a 4-5 sentence paragraph.

4.2.3 Market Needs - Market needs must be identified within the market. Every small business owner swears their target audience *needs* their product/service. But is the market ready for you? Do trends show that the market is in need of what you provide? Have you identified a social issue, an economic opportunity, or simply listened to the market trends and identified what buying behaviors are indicating at this time? Summarize your findings in a short, 4-5 sentence paragraph.

4.3 Industry Analysis

4.3.1 Main Competitors – This is the second time you will list your main competitors. Again, keep it short and simple, state what they do well for the market need and list a few weaknesses.

5.0 Web Plan Summary – Use this section to summarize all plans for your website and web marketing. Keep it short; perhaps two paragraphs of 5-6 sentences each.

5.1 Website Marketing Strategy – The website marketing strategy outlines every way you plan on using your website to market your business or run your business. Be sure to discuss SEO & PPC strategies here and any other web marketing techniques you will be incorporating.

5.2 Development Requirements – The development requirements section can be incredibly lengthy. This section outlines all the phases and releases of your technology requirements. Use visuals. This is a good place to demonstrate some of the web and technology design ideas and list out all technology and functionality requirements for any part of your product/service/market strategy for your business.

6.0 Strategy and Implementation Summary - This section of the plan describes in summary form how your company will execute the strategies, messaging, vision, and purpose to grow your brand in the community. (You can copy this sentence and use it for this section of your plan!)

6.1 Strategy Pyramid – The strategy pyramid is a visual representation of company objectives and goals. It is based on the principle that your mission, values, and vision lead the company's objectives. Additionally, it shows the importance of focus on the company's financials, strategy and execution as a team, and on an individual level.

6.2 Sales Strategy - Your sales strategy should be a multi-step process. Several sales-focuses should exist and each must have increased focus during specific periods of time during your brand building, launch, and long-term plan. The sales strategy should be summarized in table and paragraph format. This is a good time to start thinking about what type of sales personnel you will need, how they will represent you in the marketplace, and through what channels (telemarketing, networking, and/or outside sales) they will sell.

6.3 Sales Forecast – This section should include about five years of sales projections based on the data in the pro forma (will be covered in a later chapter). Write out a short paragraph that explains where the revenue is coming from, what causes increases or decreases, and what other revenue streams might come into play over time. Include a bar graph of the data for easy visual reference. Also include a one year projection with a graph and a short analysis of where your business comes from (lead source analysis; illustrate in a table).

6.4 Marketing Strategy – The marketing strategy should be the most detailed section of your business plan. Use as much detail as possible. You will reference this section hundreds of times while running and managing your business. For this specific section, simply write a summary paragraph that states your company has done a significant amount of market research through primary and secondary research methods and that you plan on using integrated marketing communications in an effort to brand your company quickly and effectively and grow your business.

6.4.1 Marketing Mix – The marketing mix refers to the 4 P's: Product, Price, Place, and Promotion (how you sell it). This section should be very detailed, use outlines, paragraphs, and bullet point lists. Here are some important notes for you on the marketing mix.

Product: clearly define your product/service. You and your company may be very good at a lot of things, but do not scare your audience by coming out of the gate with 10 different products or services. Choose one or two! Once you build brand recognition and credibility, release more products/services. DO NOT CONFUSE PRODUCTS/SERVICES WITH REVENUE STREAMS! Revenue streams are extremely important. We already discussed the fact you should have four of them. Your target audience does not need to know all the ways you make money. Most revenue streams are passive and hidden from the end user.

Price: there are two ways to price your product. Base it on market price or cost. Within market price, there are three ways to price it. Under market (means you are the Wal-Mart equivalent), at market price (means you are the JC Penney equivalent) or at above market price, or premium price (like Luis Vuitton). Each has its benefits. Choose wisely. Pricing your product/service by cost means you've calculated how much money it costs you (your company) to make/offer your product/service and you base the price on your cost + profit you'd like to make.

Place: Place refers to where you are going to sell/offer your product or service. Define this. Many small business owners have a dream of going national or global within months. For few, it is feasible. Ask yourself. Is it feasible for you? My recommendation is start within a 15 mile radius of your office. This will be helpful when you develop your promotion methods; especially if you can promote your business through networking channels, associations, and community. Start local, build your brand first. Grow when you're ready. Big dreams are good, but so is reality!

Promotion: Types of promotion methods are practically endless in today's marketing trends. Below is a short list to consider.

1) Sales and Strategic Relationships

2) Chambers/Associations
3) Launch Party/Event Hosting
4) Social Media
   a. Facebook
   b. Google
   c. Twitter
   d. Linked In
   e. You Tube
5) Traditional Methods
   a. Radio
   b. TV
   c. Magazine
   d. Print Ads
   e. Sponsorships

Develop a strategy for each of the promotional methods that pertain to your business. Remember, a certain method may not work for one market, but may work extremely well for another.

6.4.2 SWOTT Analysis - SWOTT stands for:

S – Strengths

W – Weaknesses

O – Opportunities

T – Threats

T – Trends

When you create the table, label the top columns with SWOTT. On the left hand side, label the rows with the different areas of your business. You will quickly find several areas of differentiation, areas of opportunities, knowledge/management team gaps, and market

42

opportunities (growth opportunities) for your company. I recommend including the following rows: Product/Service (list each separately), The Company, and Your Messaging & Mission. You may want to consider additional fields such as technology if it is not your main product or service and personnel, if you would like to break it out from the company section.

6.4.3 Competitive Analysis – The competitive analysis section will also be a very detailed section. You will want to elaborate on every competitor. You need to reference the competitive analysis table (mentioned earlier) to truly identify the strengths, weaknesses, opportunities, threats, and trends of your competitors. Use this section to create a clear competitive landscape. Investors will want a summary of this section; many may want to see it in detail, and it serves as a fantastic reference tool for you as you build your business. DO NOT RECREATE THE WHEEL. Your competitors are doing the right things if you're considering them competition. Study them, learn from them, and use them to create your differentiating factors. You should have at least a one page write up on each competitor. Analyze their website analytics; look at their rankings, the total monthly users, and the demographics of their audience.

6.4.4 Competitive Differentiating Factors – Use this section to write out 5-8 paragraphs on how you are different from your competition. Make a list of the differentiating factors that are relevant to your target audience, not you. Remember, they will buy what they want to buy; not necessarily what you think you sell. When writing this section, you will notice that you are now drafting marketing messages and beginning to narrow down your value proposition.

6.4.5 Marketing Messages – Before you complete this section, read through your entire plan. Read it two or three times. When you're finished, you should be able to craft 5-6 marketing messages. These messages are short. Make them one sentence each. How are you different? Why will the target audience buy from you instead of your competitors?

6.4.6 Target Market Detail - Use the target market detail section to identify in what language, tone, and style your audience needs to be spoken to for them to want to buy your product/service. Look at the competition. Are the messages happy? Sad? Fear-based? Informative? Humorous? Understanding this part is essential to your marketing plan. Use this section to write out 7-8 short paragraphs on how your target market/audience is currently being marketed to and sold to and create a brief plan within this section that describes your tone and style of messaging and why you think it will be effective.

6.5 Strategic Alliances – The strategic alliances section outlines several ways you can grow your company. Think about marshmallows as a great product and chocolate as a great product. What happened when those two great products joined forces with a third great product, graham crackers? Exactly. Think big picture here. With whom could you align down the road that could help make your company stronger, bigger, and better by forming small partnerships or joining a trifecta? List all those options here in a short, 5-6 sentence paragraph.

6.6 Value Proposition – Your value proposition is one of the most important sections of the entire plan. Without this, you really do not have a business. Trust me, we have seen it. You may build a great business, but if you cannot tell your audience why they benefit from using you or buying your product, you have little to no sales. Create a paragraph here that is one to two sentences – it should be almost identical to your mission statement.

6.7 Milestones – The milestones section is important because you can set goals for you and your business here. Think about the events that are triggers in your business. Identify benchmarks that will cause shift, change, expansion, and reasons for celebrating. Identify them now, and watch out for them!

7.0 Management Summary – The management summary is a short paragraph that lists the members, their ownership, and their involvement with the company.

7.1 Organizational Structure – Your organizational structure should be built as a representation of how business flows through the company. It is trendy to build the org chart upside down and show how important the customer is by being on top. Some companies show the structure from left to right, indicating all customers and employees are on level playing field and all have an equal importance. It is up to you how it's built, but build it with purpose and let it start creating the infrastructure for your company culture. Be sure to think of all the roles you will need to fill as the company grows. Think about capacity calculations. Example: each sales rep is responsible for bringing in 50 new clients per month. Your growth plans of new revenue should indicate how many sales reps you need to hit your objective. Additionally, you will have customer support reps handling clients. How many tiers of support reps do you need? How many managers do you need? What is everyone's capacity? When you get to 1,000 customers, you should have an equation that quickly tells you how many employees are needed to support your company growth. Think about other departments too like technology, operations, marketing, human resources, and finance.

7.2 Management Team - The management team summary is the section that allows you to include a full professional biography on everyone who is part of the management team. Investors and strategic partners may like to see who is running and behind your business. Additionally, you will be asked down the road to provide bios of your team. It is helpful to have these created on the front end so you can do some cutting and pasting when needed.

7.3 Management Team Gaps – The management team gap section is very important. Complete this truthfully. It will serve you in the long run to admit what you and your management teams' weaknesses are now. The quicker you identify what you're not great at doing, the quicker you can fill the role and be productive! Example: 80% of a startup business is sales. If you are not a natural or trained sales person, DO NOT TRY NOW! Just because you own the business and money is tight, DO NOT TRY NOW! You will throw away months of time and hundreds of dollars. Figure out where your strengths are. Leverage your strengths and fill the gaps of your weaknesses immediately. You'll save thousands of dollars in wasted time, money, and frustration. This sales rep analogy may be the biggest mistake small business owners make. There are thousands of unemployed, experience professionals in your community. Find one who can sell, offer them a commission only payment structure and performance incentive bonus plan, and let them do the selling! But this goes for all gaps; not just sales.

7.4 Personnel Plan – Use the personnel plan section to write out, in detail, what types of roles you will need. Use the same process as when you created the organization structure, but use this space to write out the plan in paragraph form, instead of a chart visual. Think about expansion and growth. It is very helpful to know your growth plan ahead of time. Do not wait until you <u>have</u> to hire someone to stay afloat. Plan and hire strategically!

This concludes sections 1.1 to 7.4 of the business plan. I recommend coming back to this chapter several times. Be sure you follow the structure and layout to build the most effective plan. Do not skip sections. I have used this format for several businesses across all different industries and sizes of companies and it has worked every time. We will discuss section 8.0, the dreaded financial projections in the next chapter.

Chapter Seven – It's Worth *How* Much?

Building financial projections can be a daunting task, but if done correctly, an accurate pro forma can be the best tool to guide decision making in your business. It is not uncommon to feel that you are not qualified to create the budget or financial projections. When we grow up, we complete years of school, yet we do not learn the standard principles of budgeting, saving, paying off debt, or investing. I have a template that is built with all the formulas needed to automatically calculate the financial projections and auto-populate your financial statements. For now, I will write out how to complete a pro forma on your own, but feel free to follow along with my template as well if you have a copy. *This template is available for download on our website.* Before you complete section 8.0, the pro forma must be built.

The first step is to complete your financial assumptions. Let us start by selecting your key performance indicators (KPIs). For a service business, KPIs can be average revenue per sale, average hourly calculated rate per service/support employee, cost per lead source (cost of acquisition), attrition rate, and capacity for service/support employee (number of customers per support rep). All these KPIs are examples; you need to find four to five KPIs that when used consistently, provide accurate data that helps you manage your business and make business decisions.

To make this clear, I will use a service business as an example. See the following table. This is the start to building our assumptions for the financial data.

KPI Description	Target
Average Revenue Per Sale	$1,000
Average Cost Per Lead	$100
Attrition Rate	20%
Average Hourly Rate (Service)	$150
Capacity per Service Rep	10 Clients

Now let us build the rest of our assumptions. Below is an example list. Some of these items may pertain to you, some may not. Create your own list.

1) The launch month is October, 2012.

2) The fiscal year is the same as the calendar year; January through December

3) Member fees are $49 per month, beginning billing in April 2013.

4) Online advertising fees begin in launch month; anticipated to be October, 2012.

    a. Fees start on a sliding scale:

        i. $99/mo. Q4 2012

        ii. $109/mo. Q1 2013

        iii. $149/mo. Q2 2013

        iv. $300/mo. 2014, $350/mo. 2015 Q1 & Q2, $400/mo. 2015 Q3 & Q4, & $450/mo. 2016 Q1 & Q2, and $500 thereafter.

5) Management team members do not take a salary until 2014. They are covered by expense reimbursement until then.

6) Web design and development fees are estimated, based on the ROM provided by the hired 3rd party technology team.

7) SEO/Pay-Per-Click/Adword fees are estimated, based on the proposal provided by the 3rd party SEO Company.

8) Consultant fees are estimated, based on the individual proposals each consultant provided for their portion of the plan.

9) Legal fees are estimated, based on the fee schedule provided by the attorney.

10) Company will operate virtually for first three to six months using shared office space and conference rooms when needed and will move into official office space by the second half of the first full year of operating.

11) Sales are estimated at 25 sales per rep per month. Best case is 45, worst case is 15.

You should now have your KPIs and your list of assumptions. It is time to start building your pro forma, which is simply a presentation of your realistic financial projections over a period of time. I always build the pro forma five years out; just to get an idea of what the potential of this company is. Most entrepreneurs like to say their projections are conservative. Studies show that whatever you put down on paper is what you'll achieve, but be realistic. Realistic projections are what should show. Those numbers should be based on market research, current trends in your market, and the market demand at your current pricing structure. Also, technology usually costs twice as much as you plan, and you should always have 3 months of rolling capital as a cushion. For all you boot-strappers out there, this exercise is vital to your growth and success.

The pro forma should have sixty months listed across the top and a yearly total column after each year. You can list as many rows as you need. I have included two examples here for this book. For boot-strapping, it's helpful to indicate which expenses can be covered by a credit card for a short term loan to yourself. The first pro forma is for an existing company that had been operating for 5 months and rebranded.

REVENUE	Jun-12	Jul-12	Aug-12	Sep-12	Oct-12
Consulting Revenue	4500	5000	5500	6500	7000
Sales Training Rev.	2500	3000	3500	4000	4500
Commission Revenue	2000	2500	3000	3500	4000
Membership Revenue	0	0	200	300	500
TOTAL	**9000**	**10500**	**12200**	**14300**	**16000**
EXPENSES					
Employee #1 Payroll	1500	1500	2500	2500	2500
Employee #1 Comm.	315	500	750	1000	1000
Employee #2 Payroll	500	500	1000	1000	100
Employee #2 Comm.	250	250	500	500	500
Employee H S A	600	600	600	600	600
Worker's Comp.	15	15	15	15	15
Accountant/Payroll	700	700	700	700	700
CC - Networking	250	250	250	250	250
CC - Radio Adv.	775	775	1000	1200	1200
CC - Phone/Internet	190	190	190	190	190
CC - Sales Database	0	390	0	0	390
CC - Meals/Entertain.	300	300	300	500	500
CC - Travel Expense	350	350	350	350	600
CC - Catering Expense	250	250	500	500	500
CC - Material Expense	157	100	100	100	100
CC - Videographer	0	700	0	0	500
CC - Website	0	2000	1500	500	500
CC - Social Media	170	500	750	750	750
Venue Expense	200	200	450	450	450
Mobile Apps	2000	50	50	50	50
SEO/PPC	500	500	500	500	600
Owner Salary	0	0	0	1000	5000
TOTAL	**9022**	**10620**	**12005**	**12655**	**16995**

PROFIT	-22	-120	195	1645	-995
Current Cash	125	($897)	($1,017)	($822)	$823
Revenue	9000	10500	12200	14300	16000
Payroll	3180	3365	5365	6615	9715
Credit Card Expenses	$2,442	$5,805	$4,940	$4,340	$5,480
Direct Expenses	3400	1450	1700	1700	1800
Outstanding CC Debt	1000				
Balance	($897)	($1,017)	($822)	$823	($172)

Because of space restrictions, this pro forma only shows five months of data. However, it shows the appropriate rows and affected cash balance. The KPIs we discussed earlier are very important here. How do you know when you need to add employee three, four, and five? What roles are they in? You can set up your pro forma to automatically begin another employee salary when you reach a certain amount of clients, as an example. Excel is a powerful tool. Each business is different from the next. Use our template or create your own, depending on the complexity of your business.

In section 8.0 of your business plan, you need to create the following:

8.0 Financial Plan – The financial plan section starts with a short summary paragraph that states a full pro forma has been completed and can be referenced at any time.

8.1 Important Assumptions - The important assumptions show here in a list format. Be sure to include all of them. The longer the list, the less room there is for interpretation with your data.

54

8.2 Key Financial Indicators – The key financial indicators are your key performance indicators. Simply write all of them out in the table format we discussed earlier in this chapter. Be sure to label each and provide a value in the second half of the chart.

8.3 Break-Even Analysis – Every investor, strategic partner, and employee should want to know when the company plans on reaching critical mass, or when it breaks even. This is when the company can actually turn a profit. Show this in both paragraph form and insert a chart or table that illustrates how many months of loss precede the month of break-even.

8.4 Projected Profit and Loss – The projected profit and loss section should include a short paragraph summary and a chart or table that illustrates this information for the first 12 months of operating.

8.5 Projected Cash Flow – Everyone wants to know how much money is in the bank! This section illustrates how much liquid cash you will have throughout the first year of operating. Good news is that we already created it. It is the bottom section of your pro forma. Simply cut and paste the first year of data into this section to show projected cash flow. This section is powerful for investors because it shows a deficit of cash due to startup expenses. You can easily add a row under "current cash" labeled investment or loan. Formulate the spreadsheet so that when you add money into this column, it populates liquid cash into your cash balance. This will help you identify how much capital you need (whether investment or loan) to stay cash positive in your business and have three months rolling capital cushion. I cannot stress how important that piece is. You cannot control all the factors in your business. You must have a three month cushion! Technology may break, you may need to hire an employee earlier than expected, and you may have completely bombed on a project, or lost your biggest client.   Always have three months saved up and available to access!

8.6 Pro Forma – Simply state one more time that you have a full pro forma available to view should any investor or strategic partner need to see it.

8.7 Exit Strategy – Every business owner must begin with the end in mind! You should know from the beginning if this is a three year, five year, ten year, or pass-down-to-family, type of business. Most companies now sell within three to five years; especially in the tech business. Most services-based companies still last about five to ten years. Very rarely are businesses being built that are planning on being passed down through the family; generation after generation. The exit strategy should be very detailed. It should explain who the main players are in the company at the management team level, who plans on working in what role, who plans on stepping aside after a certain amount of time, what the succession plan is, who a potential buyer of the company would be, in what time frame would the company start looking for buyers (what milestones need to be hit, as an example), and/or go IPO. These are several examples of the questions you should ask yourself. A company can take two to three years to sell. Be sure you discuss this strategy with your attorney, accountant, and other management team members.

Chapter Eight – The Perfect Representation

Completing the executive summary can be difficult because you now have to summarize 50 pages worth of information from your plan into a two page summary. When completing the executive summary, follow these tips and it should be a painless process.

Below are the items that should be included:

1) **Company Information**
2) **Products/Services**
3) **The Market**
4) **The Competition**
5) **Financial Considerations**
6) **Management Team Information**
7) **Contact Information**

Executive summaries should include color, graphs, charts, and box sections for easy-to-follow reading. *We have templates available for you to use on our website,* or you can create your own.

On the front page of the executive summary, we recommend placing your company logo in the top right section of the document. Don't have a logo yet? Try a company like 99designs.com. Secondly, create a colored side bar down the left-hand side of the page. Use this bar to include information like company name, location, website address, year founded, mission statement, product/service bullet-point list, company summary and market summary. A side bar example has been included next.

COMPANY NAME

FOUNDED: 2010
HEADQUARTERS: Chicago, IL
WEBSITE: www.company.com

MISSION: Insert your mission statement here; be sure to include the messaging that relates to what you plan on accomplishing by creating this company.

COMPANY: This is the short paragraph you created that belongs in section 1.0 of the business plan, You can cut and paste into this section.

PRODUCTS/SERVICES/REVENUE STREAMS:
- Product/Service #1
- Product/Service #2
- Product/Service #3
- Hidden Revenue Stream

MARKET: Review your market analysis summary and write a 3-4 sentence paragraph here that accurately sums up your current market and potential market growth based on your research that works in your company's favor for expansion and success.

CONTACT INFORMATION:
YOUR NAME HERE,TITLE
888-555-5555
Yourname@company.com

The right-hand section of your executive summary should be three charts/graphs. Use color and clean graphics/visuals! The three charts/graphs include:

1) Financial Highlights (five years of revenue, expenses, and profit shown in a chart ← from pro forma)
2) Sales Forecast Year One (first year of sales revenue; show by lead source if possible ← from pro forma)
3) Startup Expenses Table (from pro forma)

If you're seeking an investment or loan, change out the second chart/graph to show "use of funds". Then startup expenses table will indicate how much money you need to start the company. Complete a "used of funds" pie chart to illustrate where a potential investment would be allocated. Below is an example.

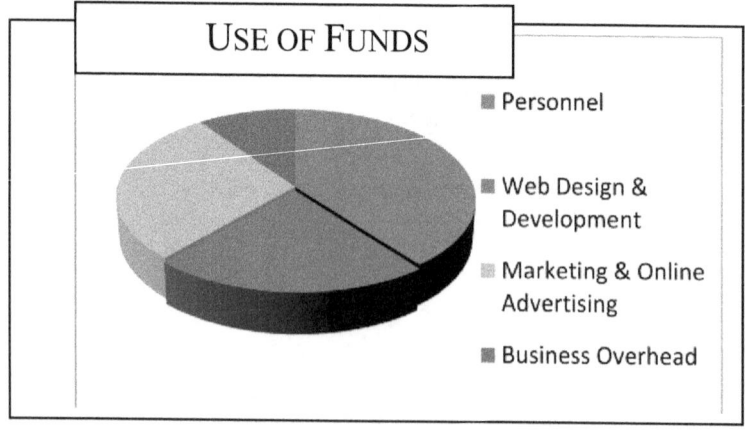

REQUEST OF FUNDS		
Total Startup Expenses	$1,200,000	
Total Estimated Revenue	$400,000	
Capital Cushion Account	$200,000	
Required Funding	$1,000,000	$1M

USE OF FUNDS

- Personnel
- Web Design & Development
- Marketing & Online Advertising
- Business Overhead

The second page (reverse side of the document) should contain box sections and illustrate with paragraphs, bullet-points, and graphics/visuals the following information:

1) Competitive Landscape
2) Differentiating Factors
3) Management Team Summary

This information needs to be clear, concise and presented in a tone that is easy to follow and understand. When creating messaging for your company, always remember you know too much! You must write all your messaging in the tone and style that your audience will understand the best. Use this process, even with the executive summary.

Chapter Nine – So Now What?

Education without action is simply entertainment. Ask yourself what your next step is to building your business. I cannot answer that for you. Everyone who reads this book is at a different stage in their business. Some are brand new, some are rebranding. Once your plan is built, start executing. I recommend branding yourself immediately. Use your social media outlets to update your personal profiles. Buy your domain name for your website and get it built! Start building a web presence, because that is where people will look first! Everyone can do their homework these days on the Internet. It is your opportunity to brand yourself. How do you want people to see you? As a professional? Approachable? Knowledgeable? Credible? You get to choose. Use the messaging tips we discuss and start branding yourself immediately. Create your business cards with a purpose. Most business cards are either thrown into the trash or added to a stack that is never touched. What will make yours stand out?

If you are a brand new business, hire an accountant to file your paperwork with the state and IRS. They know what needs to be done. Do research on what bank to bank with. Many have great programs for businesses; especially new ones. Start looking into chambers, associations, and community events to begin promoting you and your concept. Build a network and a following that like, know, and trust you. The quicker you build your network, the more fans you'll have to support your launch and help you spread the word. Make connections the right way. This is about quality, not quantity. Mass numbers of followers and connections will make you play the numbers game and it will be a waste of your time down the road.

Create a packet about your business that you can carry in your car. Create a branded series of information: business card, two-page info slick, full marketing brochure, and always have the most recent copy of your business plan with you. I recommend creating a branded folder as well to carry your items in. It just adds that much more to your overall appearance and look. You are in such a lucky spot – you get to create the appearance of who you have always wanted to be in business and in this marketplace. Look the part! Speak the part! Be the part!

Once you begin these steps, identify your team members. Do not hire the first person you 'like'. Create a hiring process. Know your "knock-out" factors. Employees and contractors must share your values, ethics, and morals. They must share your vision and be excited about your company. Do not hire someone who is simply looking for a job. Build a team of committed individuals who believe in you, support you, and want to see you succeed. They will know when you succeed, they succeed.

As soon as your team is in place, build a meeting structure. Set meetings up on a recurring schedule and make them mandatory. Set an agenda for each meeting. Stick to the agenda. Respect everyone's time; don't run over. Set clear expectations for objectives, quotas, activity, and goals. Answer questions. Create your culture and environment immediately. Follow your plan!

Now is your time to shine. Build your business worth owning. Stick to your plan and timeline. Follow your timeline for creating technology, systems and processes. Begin your marketing campaign and sales cycle. Begin working with customers/clients. Constantly ask them for feedback. Incorporate their feedback! Listen to your employees. Ask them for feedback. Incorporate their feedback!

I will end this book by sharing some key points with you about running a business. These are business tips I have read or heard along the way, and I think they all have value.

- **Do you own your business, or does your business own you?**
- **Did you create a business, or did you create a place of employment for yourself?**
- **What would happen to your business if you got hit by a bus?**
- **Do you want your employees to like you or be inspired by you?**
- **Do your employees understand how every action they make affects your bottom-line?**
- **What is your average hourly calculated rate? How much money do you lose on a weekly basis conducting or performing tasks that are not your strength or in your job description?**
- **Understand your worth. Remove any poverty complex you might have and take some medication so you're not allergic to money anymore. Ask for money. Ask for the business.**
- **Avoid unpaid consulting. This typically happens in a sales process.**
- **You do not need to have coffee with everyone. Be selective on who you meet with and why. Remember, you have an hourly rate. Every coffee meeting you set must present some type of opportunity for you or your business. You do not**

make money by having coffee with everyone who wants to get to know you.

- You have a life. Build your business into it. Do you run your business or does your business run you?
- Thank people. Thank them often and genuinely. Show appreciation and gratitude through verbal, social, virtual, physical, and service methods.
- People buy from people they know, like, and trust.

Please send your comments or questions to:

Mary MacNeilly
The Butterfly Creative

Via our request form, accessible at:

www.thebutterflycreative.com